That Is Math!

Betsy Franco
Illustrated by Christine Powers

Rigby

Look in this room.
Where do you
see math?

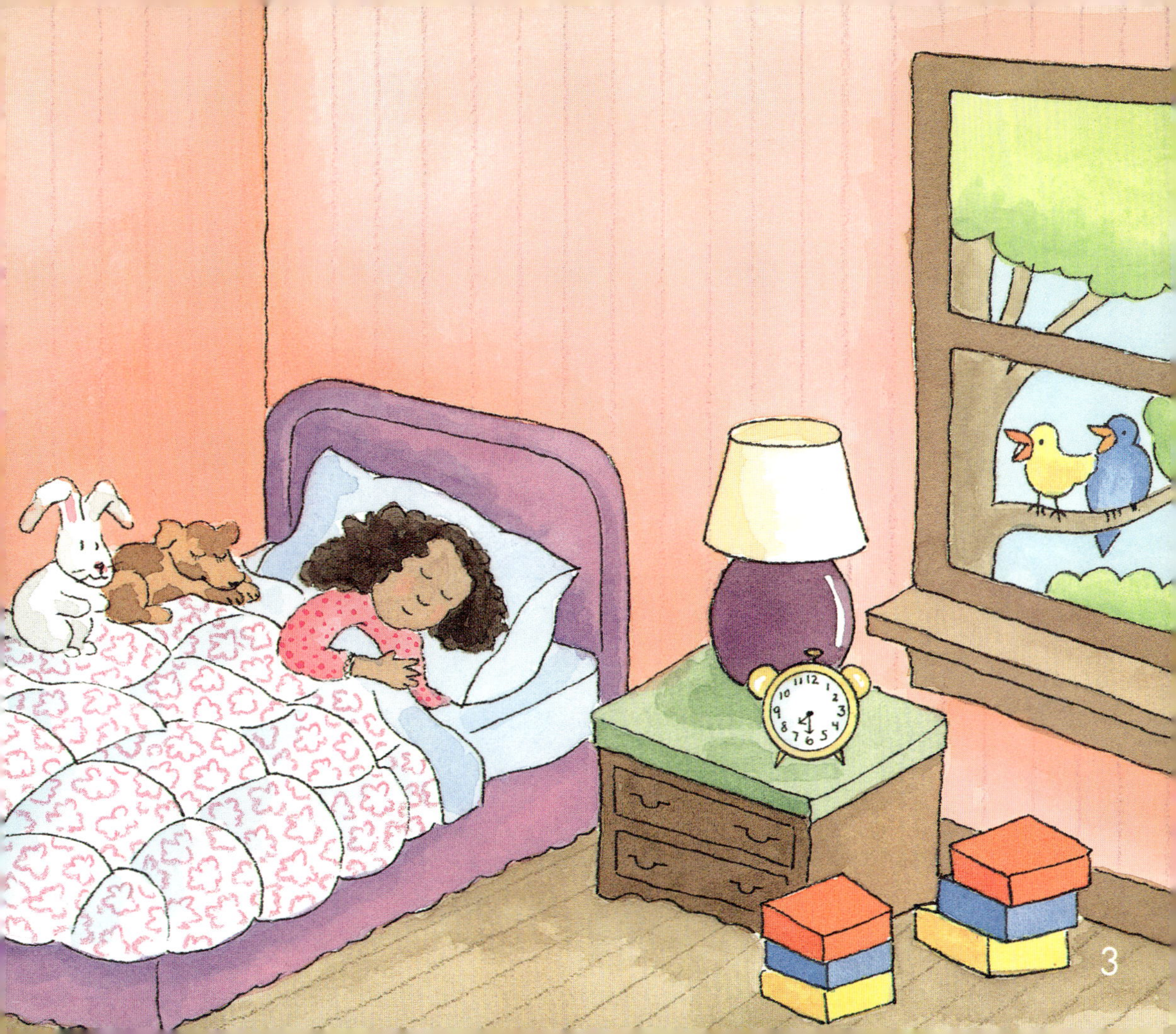

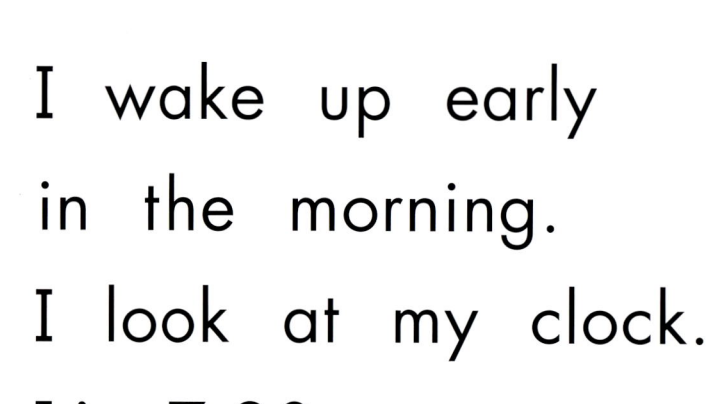

I wake up early
in the morning.
I look at my clock.
It's 7:30.

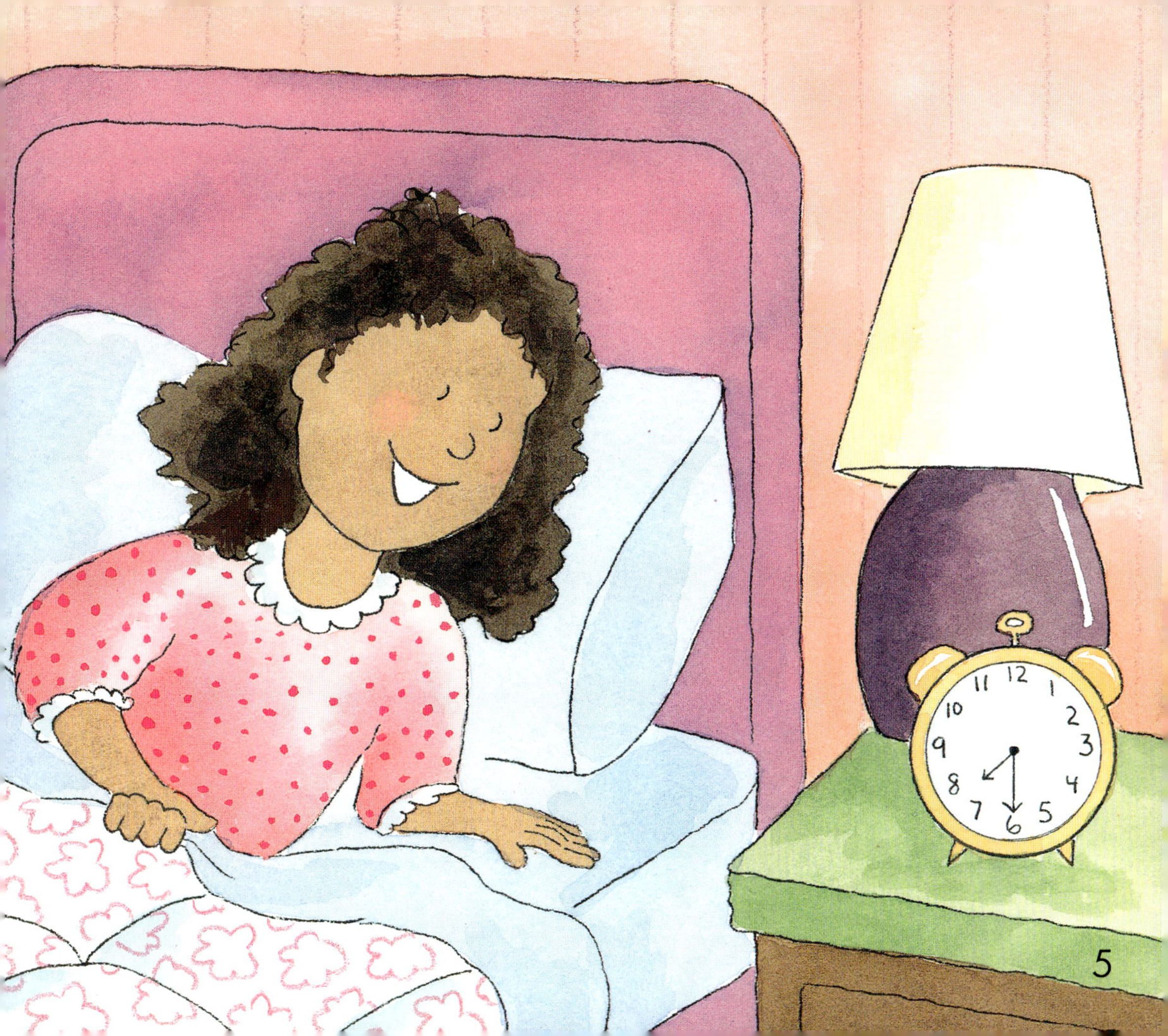
12 1 2 3 4 5 6 7 8 9 10 11

The time is 7:30.
That is math!

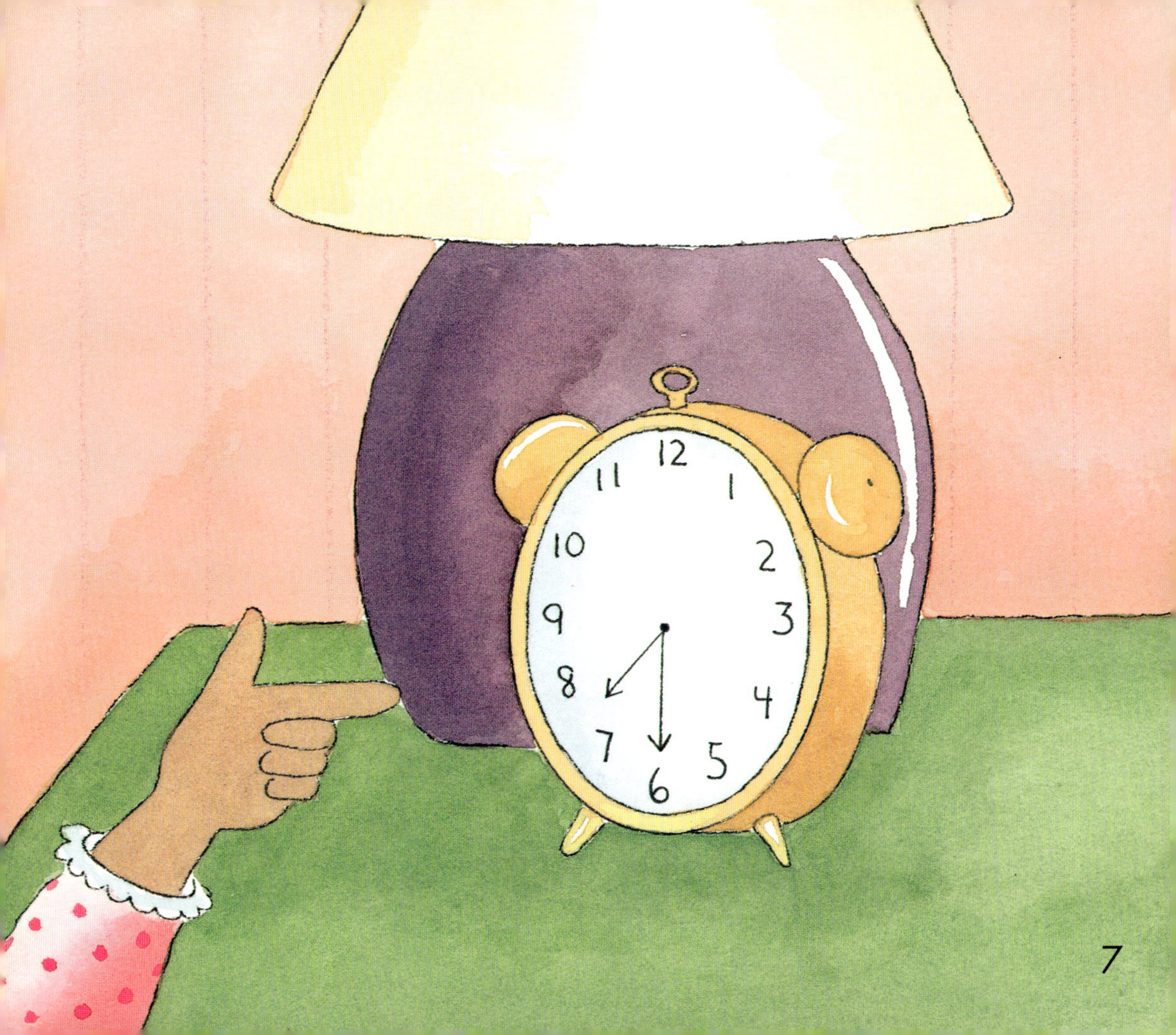
12
1
2
3
4
5
6
7
8
9
10
11

I want
to eat breakfast.
My mom makes
three pancakes.
I love pancakes!

9

I eat two pancakes.
My brother eats one pancake.
That is math, too!

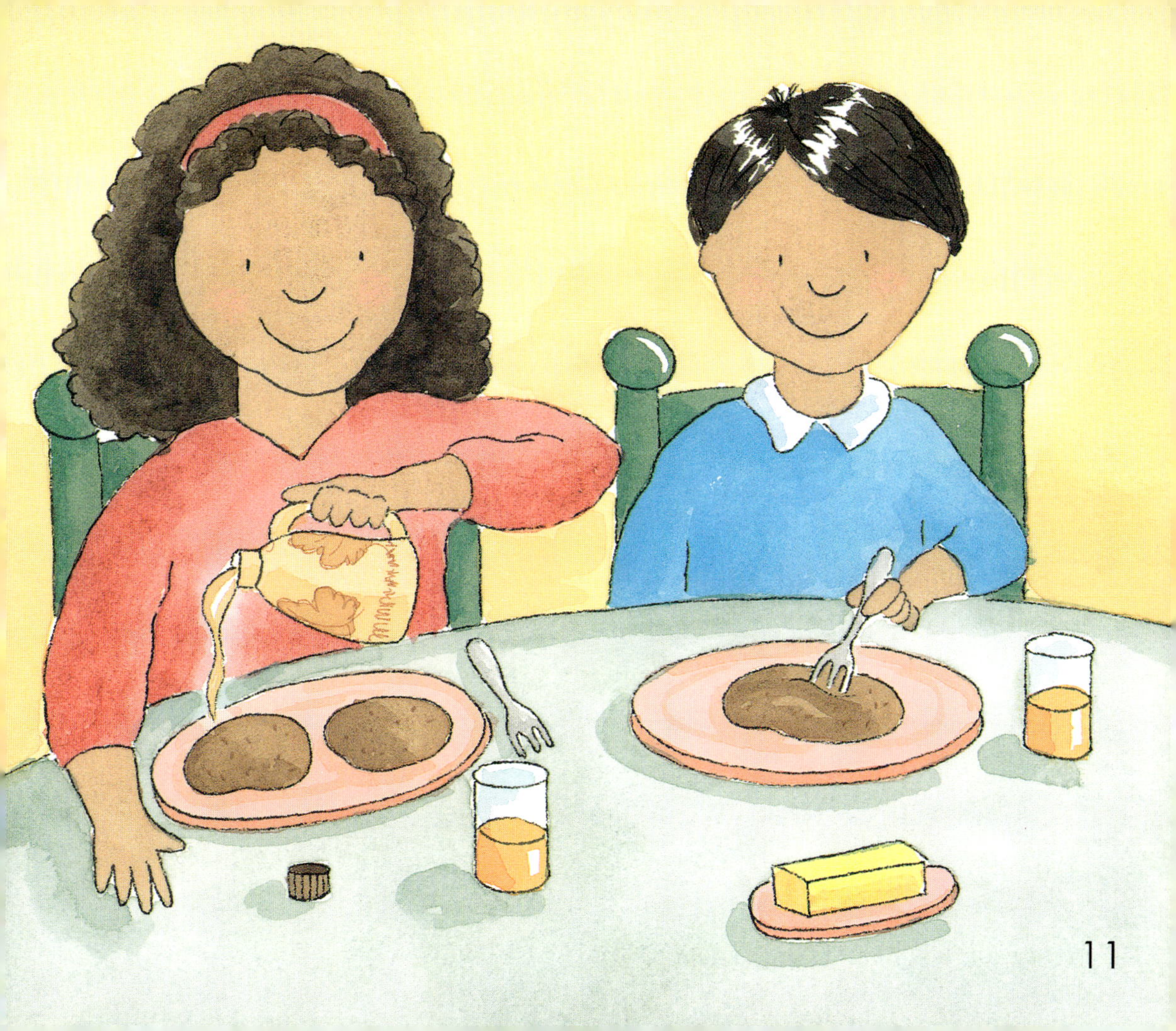

Mom has one dollar.
She gives us money
for lunch and milk.

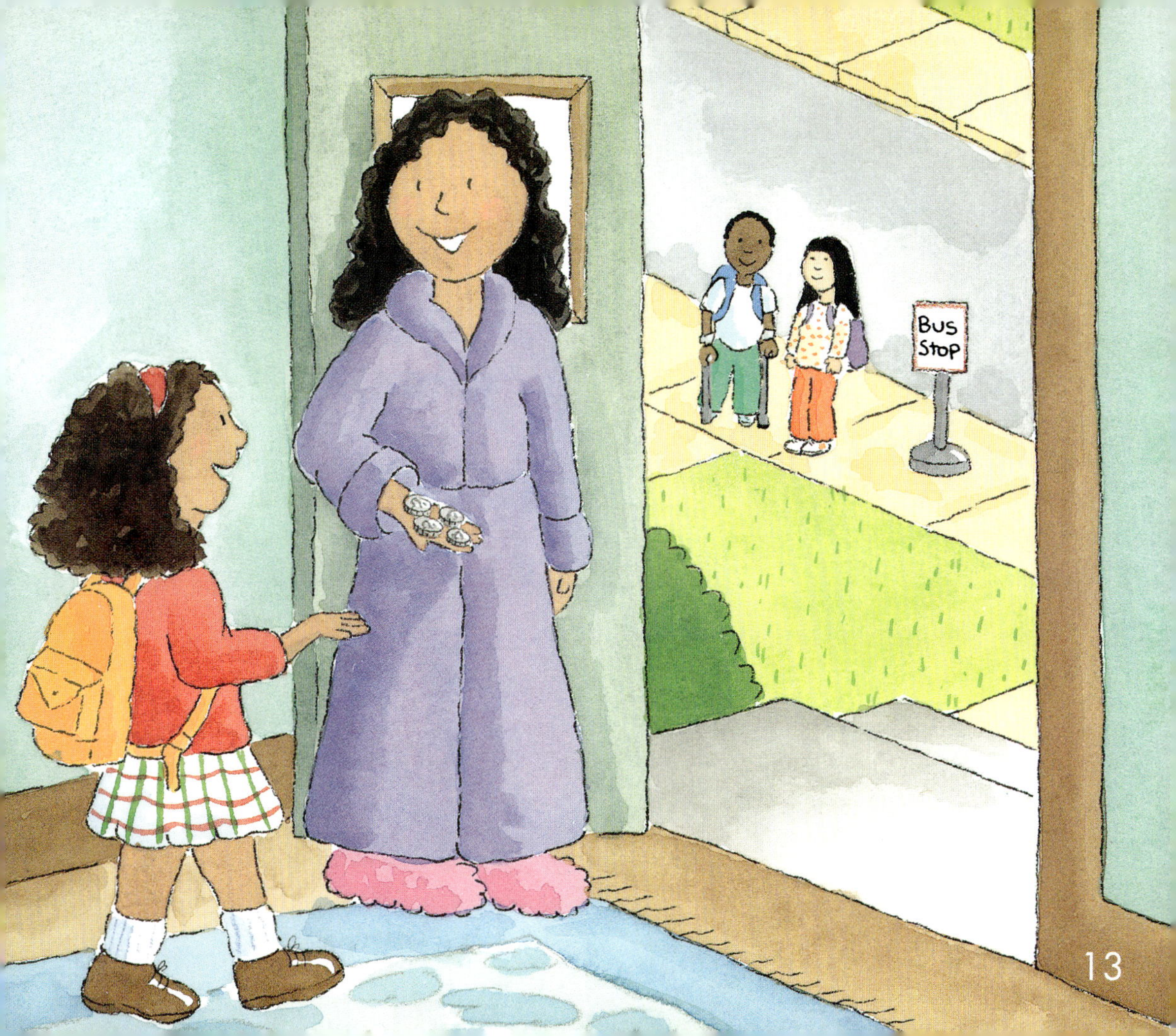
Bus Stop

We each get two coins.
That is math, too!

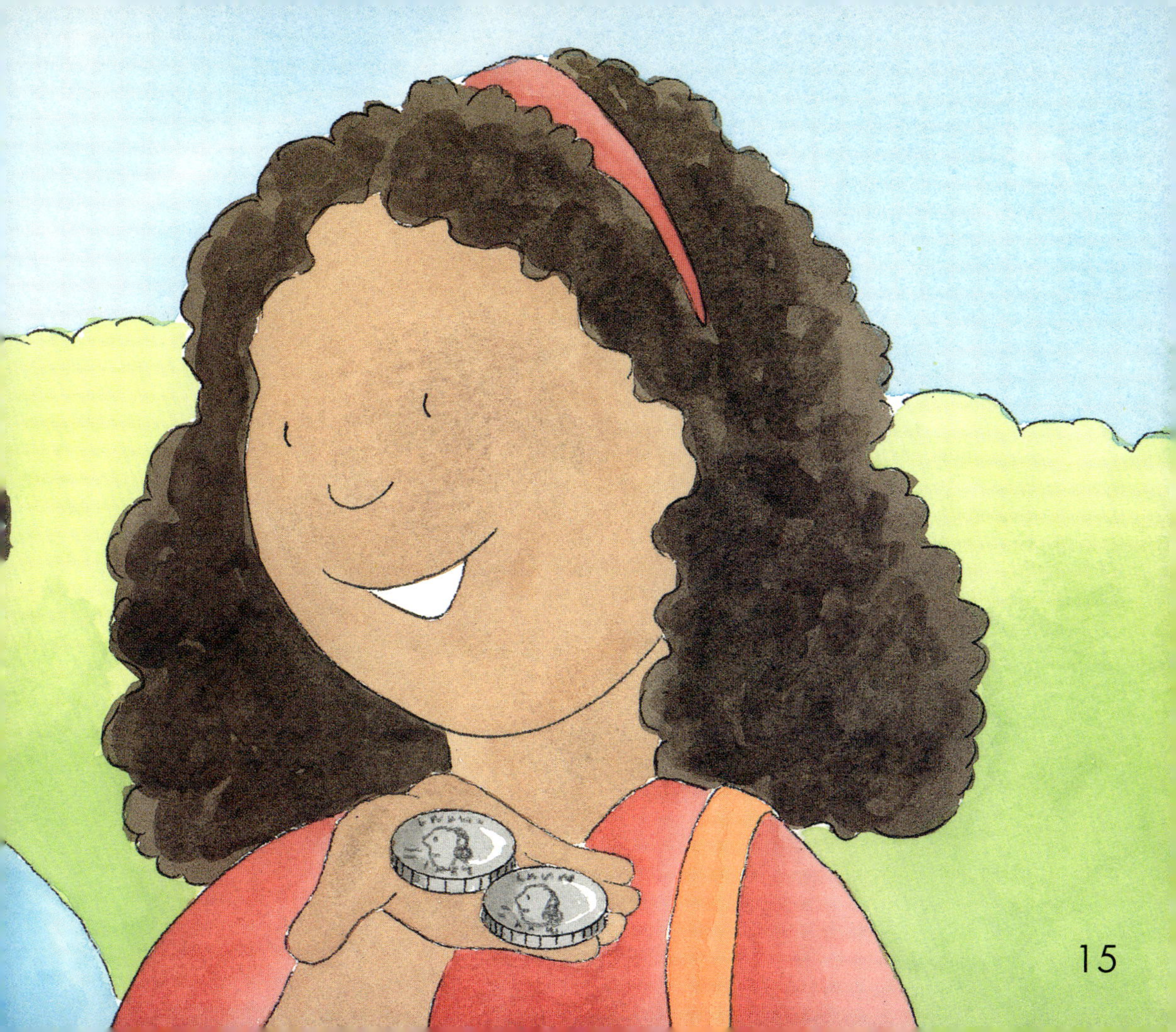

We walk to the bus stop.
I see math all over. Do you?